My Biling   ...
Talking Dictionary

Cantonese & English

MANTRA LINGUA
Listen, record, playback...

TalkingPEN™

First published in 2005 by Mantra Lingua
Global House, 303 Ballards Lane, London N12 8NP
www.mantralingua.com

This TalkingPEN edition 2009
Text copyright © 2005 Mantra Lingua
Illustrations copyright © 2005 Mantra Lingua
(except pages 4-9, 42-49 Illustrations copyright © 2005 Priscilla Lamont)
Audio copyright © 2009 Mantra Lingua

With thanks to the illustrators:
David Anstey, Dixie Bedford-Stockwell, Louise Daykin,
Alison Hopkins, Richard Johnson, Allan Jones,
Priscilla Lamont, Yokococo

A CIP record for this book is available from the British Library

Hear each page of this talking book narrated with the RecorderPEN!

1) To get started touch the arrow button below with the RecorderPEN.

2) To hear the word in English touch the 'E' button at the top of the pages.

3) To hear the word spoken in an English sentence touch the 'S' button at the top of the pages.

4) To hear the language of your choice touch the 'L' button on the top of the pages.

5) Touch the square button below to hear more information about using the Dictionary with the RecorderPEN.

Start   Information

Contents

Myself

眼睛
aan jing
eyes

頭髮
tou faat
hair

口
hou
mouth

耳
yi dor
ears

牙齒
aar chi
teeth

手
shou
hand

手指公
shou zhi gung
thumb

手腕
shou woon
wrist

手指
shou zhi
fingers

腰
yiu
waist

腳
ghur
feet

腳趾
ghur zhi
toes

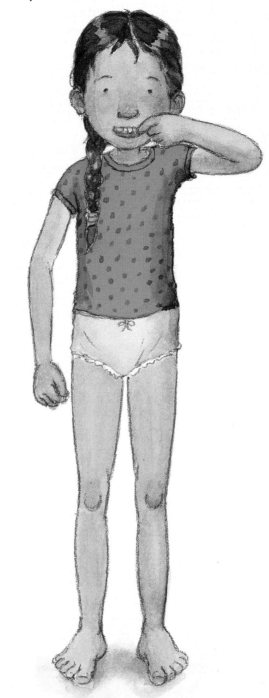

快樂
fai lok
happy

悲傷
bei sheung
sad

憤怒
fun loh
angry

妒忌
doh gei
jealous

興奮
hing fun
excited

4

面
meen
face

頭
tou
head

自己

鼻子
bei zi
nose

頸
gang
neck

手臂
shou bei
arm

膊頭
bo tou
shoulders

胃
wei
stomach

手肘
shou zhaang
elbow

膝頭
shut tou
knee

背部
bui boh
back

腳眼
ghur aan
ankle

腿
tui
leg

有病
yao beng
sick

肚餓
tow or
hungry

害怕
hoi pa
scared

怕醜
pa chou
shy

疲倦
pei guen
tired

Clothes

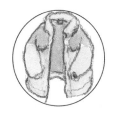

外套
oil toh
coat

頸巾
gang gun
scarf

t-恤
t-suut
t-shirt

全身裙
chuun shen kuan
dress

半截裙
boon jeet kuan
skirt

冷外套
leng oil toh
cardigan

游泳衣
yao wing yi
swimming costume

襪褲
mut fu
tights

内褲
noi fu
knickers

鞋
hai
shoes

衣服

手套
shou toh
gloves

帽
moh
hat

恤衫
suut shaam
shirt

冷衫
leng shaam
jumper

褲
fu
trousers

短褲
duen fu
shorts

游泳褲
yao wing fu
swimming trunks

襪
mut
socks

内褲
noi fu
underpants

運動鞋
won dung hai
trainers

7

Family

家庭成員

祖母
jo moh
grandmother

祖父
jo fu
grandfather

外公
oi gung
grandfather

外婆
oi po
grandmother

姑媽
gu ma
aunt

爸爸
ba ba
father

媽媽
ma ma
mother

舅父
kou fu
uncle

兄弟
hing dai
brother

姐妹
jeh mui
sister

仔
zai
son

女
lui
daughter

啤啤
bee bee
baby

Home

家居

屋頂
oak deng
roof

屋頂室
oak deng sut
attic

窗
cheung
window

浴室
yok sut
bathroom

睡房
sui fong
bedroom

飯廳
faan teng
dining room

廚房
chu fong
kitchen

門廳
mun teng
hallway

牆壁
cheung bik
wall

大廳
dai ting
lounge/living room

樓梯間
lou tai gaan
staircase

門
mun
door

House and Contents

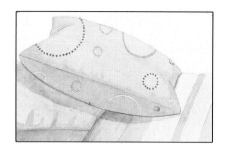

枕頭
jump tou
pillow

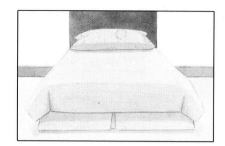

床
chong
bed

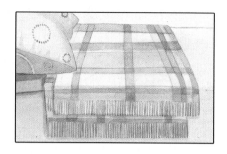

毛氈
mo jeen
blanket

垃圾桶
laap saap tung
bin

風扇
fung seen
fan

燈
deng
lamp

電話
deen wa
telephone

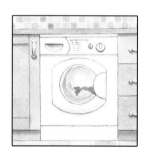

洗衣機
sai yi gei
washing machine

烘麵包爐
hong meen bao loh
toaster

水煲
shui bo
kettle

水喉
sui hou
tap

雪櫃
suut guai
fridge

煮食爐
zhu sik loh
cooker

洗碗盤
sai woon puun
sink

散熱器
saan yit hei
radiator

浴缸
yok gong
bath

毛巾
moh gun
towel

鏡
geng
mirror

廁所
chi soh
toilet

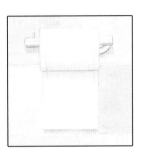

廁紙
chi zi
toilet roll

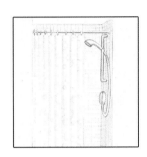

花洒
fa sa
shower

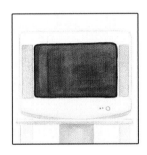

電視機
deen si gei
television

收音機
shou yum gei
radio

窗簾
cheung leem
curtains

櫥櫃
chu guai
cupboard

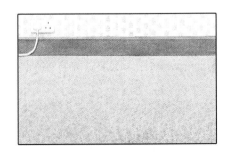

地氈
dei jeen
carpet

梳發
shuo fa
sofa

檯
toi
table

Fruit

香蕉
heung jiu
banana

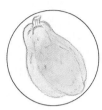

木瓜
muk gua
papaya

雪梨
suut lei
pear

蜜瓜
mut gua
melon

李
lei
plum

檸檬
ling mung
lemon

車厘子
che lei zi
cherries

士多啤李
si duo beh lei
strawberries

水果

提子
tai zi
grapes

菠蘿
bo loh
pineapple

芒果
mong goh
mango

橙
chaarn
orange

桃
tow
peach

蘋果
ping goh
apple

荔枝
lai zhi
lychees

石榴
sek lou
pomegranate

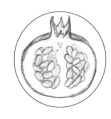

Vegetables

洋蔥
yeung chong
onion

椰菜花
yeh choi fa
cauliflower

薯仔
shu zai
potato

粟米
sook mai
sweetcorn

蘑菇
mor gu
mushroom

蕃茄
faan kieh
tomato

豆角
dou goh
beans

蘿蔔
loh baak
radish

蒜頭
suun tou
garlic

南瓜
laam gua
pumpkin/squash

青瓜
cheng gua
cucumber

西蘭花
si laan fa
broccoli

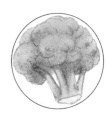

青紅椒
cheng hung jiu
pepper/capsicum

紅蘿蔔
hung loh baak
carrot

生菜
sang choi
lettuce

青豆
cheng dou
peas

15

Food and Drink

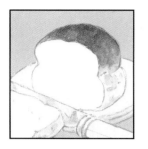

麵包

meen bao

bread

牛油

ao yao

butter

果醬

goh jeung

jam

三文治

saam mun zhi

sandwich

糖

tong

sugar

蜜糖

mut tong

honey

穀類食品

gok lui sik bun

cereal

牛奶

ao nai

milk

麵

meen

noodles

飯/米

faan(cooked rice)\mai(uncooked rice)

rice

意大利粉

yi dai lei fun

spaghetti

意大利薄餅

yi dai lei bok beng

pizza

肉類

yuuk lui

meat

魚

yu

fish

蛋

daan

egg

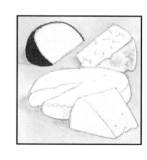

芝士

ji si

cheese

朱古力
zhu gu lik
chocolate

糖果
tong goh
sweets

蛋糕
daan goh
cake

布甸
boh deen
pudding

乳酸
yu suen
yoghurt

雪糕
suut goh
ice cream

餅乾
beng gone
biscuit

薯片
shu peen
crisps

薯條
shu til
chips

茄汁
kieh jup
ketchup

芥辣
gai lard
mustard

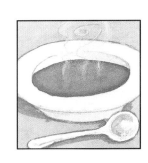

湯
tong
soup

果汁
goh jup
fruit juice

礦泉水
kong chuen sui
mineral water

鹽
yeem
salt

胡椒粉
wu jiu fun
pepper

Meal Time

刀
dou
knife

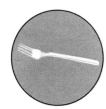

叉
cha
fork

匙羹
chi geng
spoon

筷子
fai zi
chopsticks

大杯
dai bui
mug

茶杯
cha bui
cup

玻璃杯
bo lei bui
glass

食飯時間

碟
diep
plate

碗
woon
bowl

平底煲
ping dai bo
saucepan

鑊
wok
wok

煎鑊
jeen wok
frying pan

暖壺
luan wu
flask

飯盒
faan hup
lunchbox

Town

超級市場
chiu cup si cheung
supermarket

停車場
ting che cheung
car park

運動中心
wun dung zhong sum
sports centre

圖書館
toh shu guun
library

警署
geng chu
police station

火車站
four che zhaam
train station

消防局
siu fong guk
fire station

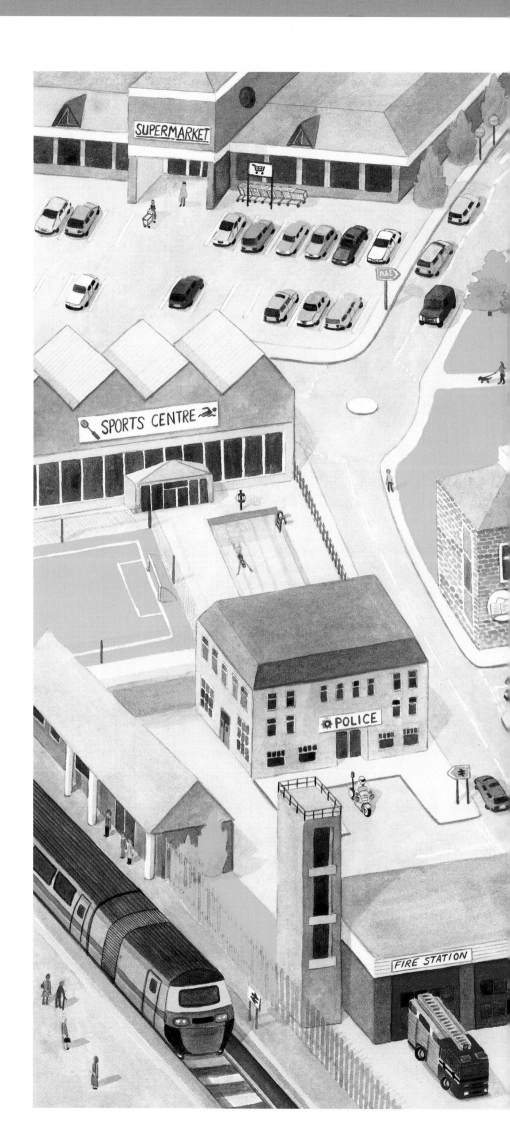

醫院
yi yuen
hospital

公園
gong yuen
park

戲院
hei yuen
cinema

汽車修理站
hei che sao lei zhaam
garage

巴士站
ba si zhaam
bus station

商店
sheung deem
shops/stores

學校
hok hao
school

High Street

餐廳
chaan teng
restaurant

花店
fa deem
florist

報紙攤
bo zi taan
newspaper stand

書店
shu deem
book shop

肉店
yuuk deem
butcher

郵局
yao guuk
post office

魚販
yu faan
fishmonger

蔬菜水果商
sor choi sui goh sheung
greengrocer

藥房
yerk fong
chemist

麵包舖
meen bao po
bakery

銀行
aarn hong
bank

玩具店
woon gui deem
toyshop

咖啡室
ga feh sut
coffee shop

美容理髮師
mei yung lei faat si
hairdressers

Road Safety

馬路
ma loh
road

交通燈
gao tung deng
traffic light

紅人燈號
hung yen deng hao
red man

綠人燈號
look yen deng hao
green man

車燈
che deng
lights

反射器
faan she hei
reflector

單車頭盔
daan che tou kuai
cycle helmet

人行橫渡線
yen heng huaan doh seen
pedestrian crossing

前進
cheen jun
go

停步
ting bo
stop

觀察
guun chaat
look

聆聽
ling ting
listen

兒童橫渡線
yi tong huaan doh seen
children crossing

學校馬路督察
hok hao ma loh duuk cha
school crossing patrol officer

安全帶
on chuen dai
seat belt

人行道
yen heng doh
pavement

Transport

飛機
fei gei
aeroplane

貨車
four che
lorry/truck

汽車
hei che
car

長途旅遊巴士
cheung tow lui yao ba si
coach

小船
siu suen
boat

單車
daan che
bicycle

火車
four che
train

電單車
deen daan che
motorbike

直升機
jik xing gei
helicopter

巴士
ba si
bus

電車
deen che
tram

旅遊住屋車
lui yao zhu oak che
caravan

大船
dai suen
ship

人力車
yen lik che
rickshaw

Farm Animals

雀鳥
jerk niu
bird

馬
ma
horse

鴨
aarp
duck

貓
mao
cat

山羊
saan yeung
goat

兔子
toe zi
rabbit

狐狸
wu lei
fox

農場動物

牛
ao
cow

狗
gou
dog

羊
yeung
sheep

老鼠
loh shu
mouse

雞
gai
hen

驢
loh
donkey

鵝
orr
goose

Wild Animals

猴子
hou zi
monkey

大笨象
dai bun jeung
elephant

蛇
se
snake

斑馬
baan ma
zebra

獅子
si zi
lion

河馬
hoh ma
hippopotamus

海豚
hoi tuen
dolphin

鯨魚
king yu
whale

野生動物

熊貓
hung mao
panda bear

長頸鹿
cheung geng luuk
giraffe

駱駝
lok tor
camel

老虎
loh fu
tiger

熊
hung
bear

企鵝
kei orr
penguin

鱷魚
orc yu
crocodile

鯊魚
sa yu
shark

Seaside

海
hoi
sea

海浪
hoi long
waves

沙灘
sa taan
beach

救生員
gou saang yuen
lifeguard

太陽油
tai yeung yao
sun lotion

貝殼
bui hok
shells

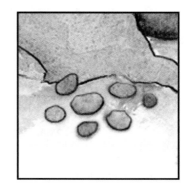

卵石
luun sek
pebbles

海藻
hoi cho
seaweed

水灘
sui taan
rock pool

蟹
hai
crab

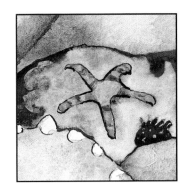

星魚
xing yu
starfish

帆布椅
faan bao yi
deckchair

沙
sa
sand

沙城堡
sa sing bo
sandcastle

桶
tung
bucket

鏟
chaan
spade

Playground

鞦韆

chou cheen

swing

團團轉

tuen tuen zhuen

roundabout

搖搖板

yiu yiu baan

seesaw

沙池

sa chi

sandpit

隧道

sui doh

tunnel

裏面

lui meen

in

外面

oil meen

out

跳繩

til xing

skip

攀架
paan ga
climbing frame

向上
heung sheung
up

滑梯
waat tigh
slide

向下
heung ha
down

在上面
joy sheung meen
over

在下面
joy ha meen
under

前面
cheen meen
in front

後面
hou meen
behind

The Classroom

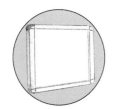

白板
baak baan
white board

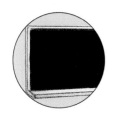

黑板
haark baan
chalk board

書檯
shu toi
desk

椅子
yi zi
chair

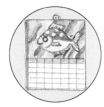

日曆
yut lik
calendar

錄音機
look yum gei
tape recorder

錄音盒帶
look yum hup dai
cassette tape

計數機
gai so gei
calculator

教室

教師
gao si
teacher

書本
shu boon
books

紙
zi
paper

顏色
aan sik
paint

畫筆
wa butt
paintbrush

較剪
gao jeen
scissors

膠水
gao sui
glue

膠紙
gao zi
sticky tape

School Bag

寫字簿
she zi bo
writing book

數學書
so hok shu
maths book

文件夾
mun geen garp
folder

尺
chek
ruler

量角器
leung gok hei
protractor

鉛筆
yuen butt
pencil

鉛筆刨
yuen butt pao
pencil sharpener

閱讀書本
yuet duk shu boon
reading book

蠟筆
laap butt
crayon

繩
xing
string

錢
chien
money

圓規
yuen kuai
compass

膠擦
gao chaat
rubber/eraser

水筆
sui butt
felt tip pen

Computers

掃描器
so miu hei
scanner

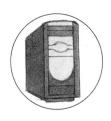

電腦
deen nao
computer

展示器
jeen shi hei
monitor

鍵盤
geen poon
keyboard

滑鼠
waat shu
mouse

滑鼠墊
waat shu jeen
mouse mat

電腦

打印機
da yun gei
printer

屏幕
ping mok
screen

互聯網
wu luen mong
internet

電子郵件
deen zi yao geen
email

光碟
guang diep
cd disc

軟式磁碟
yuen sek chi diep
floppy disc

Dressing Up

太空人
tai hung yen
astronaut

警察
geng cha
police person

獸醫
sou yi
vet

消防員
siu fong yuen
firefighter

畫家
wa ga
artist

商店老闆
sheung deem lo baan
shop keeper

賽馬騎師
choi ma keh si
jockey

牛仔
ao zai
cowboy

廚師
chu si
chef

護士
wu si
nurse

汽車修理技工
hei che sao lei gei gung
mechanic

火車司機
four che si gei
train driver

芭蕾舞蹈員
ba lei mo doh yuen
ballet dancer

流行歌星
lao heng goh xing
pop star

小丑
siu chou
clown

海盜
hoi doh
pirate

巫師
mo si
wizard

醫生
yi seng
doctor

Toys and Games

氣球
hei kou

balloon

珠
zhu

beads

棋盤遊戲
kei poon yao hei

board game

洋娃娃
yeung wa wa

doll

洋娃娃之家
yeung wa wa zhi ga

doll's house

風箏
fung zheng

kite

智商遊戲
ji sheung yao hei

puzzle

跳繩
til xing

skipping rope

陀螺
tor lor

spinning top

積木
jik muk
building blocks

國際象棋
goh jai jeung kei
chess

骰子
sik zi
dice

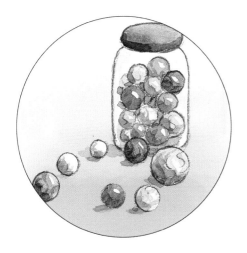

波子
bo zi
marbles

紙牌
zi pai
playing cards

木偶
muk ou
puppet

玩具熊
woon gui hung
teddy bear

模型火車
mo ying four che
train set

玩具汽車
woon gui hei che
toy car

Sport

籃球
laam kou
basketball

波
bo
ball

板球
baan kou
cricket

羽毛球
yu mao kou
badminton

游泳
yao wing
swimming

滾軸鞋
guun zhuk hai
roller skates

球拍
kou paak
racquet

溜冰鞋
lao bing hai
ice skates

網球
mong kou
tennis

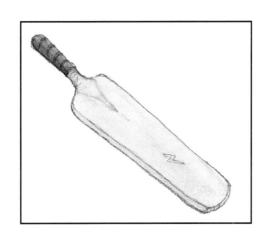

板球棒
baan kou paang
bat

網籃球
mong laam kou
netball

足球
zhuk kou
football

騎單車
keh daan che
cycling

欖球
laam kou
rugby

滑板
waat baan
skateboard

曲棍球
kuk guun kou
hockey

Music

鼓
gu
drum

印度鼓
yun doh gu
tabla

單簧管
daan wong guun
clarinet

簫
siu
flute

豎琴
shu kum
harp

琴鍵盤
kum geen poon
keyboard

結他
geet ta
guitar

樂譜架
org po ga
music stand

三角
saam gok
musical triangle

喇叭
la ba
trumpet

響葫蘆
heung wu lo
maracas

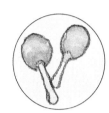

非洲鼓
fei zhou gu
gan gan

鋼琴
gong kum
piano

直笛
jik dec
recorder

小提琴
siu tei kum
violin

木琴
muk kum
xylophone

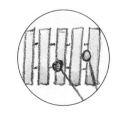

Space

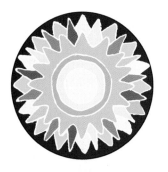

太陽
tai yeung
sun

水星
sui xing
Mercury

金星
gum xing
Venus

地球
dei kou
Earth

月亮
yuet leung
moon

太空船
tai hung suen
spaceship

流星
lao xing
shooting star

火箭
four jeen
rocket

火星
four xing
Mars

木星
muk xing
Jupiter

土星
tow xing
Saturn

天王星
teen wong xing
Uranus

彗星
sui xing
comet

星星
xing xing
stars

海王星
hoi wong xing
Neptune

冥王星
ming wong xing
Pluto

Weather

晴朗
ching long
sunny

彩虹
choi hung
rainbow

落雨
lok yu
rainy

雷
lui
thunder

閃電
seem deen
lightning

暴風雨
bo fung yu
stormy

大風
dai fung
windy

籠霧
lung mo
foggy

落雪
lok suut
snowy

天陰有雲
teen yum yao wun
cloudy

冰雹
bing bok
hail

冰冷
bing laang de
icy

Months of the Year

月份

一月
yut yuet
January

二月
yi yuet
February

三月
saam yuet
March

四月
sei yuet
April

五月
um yuet
May

六月
luk yuet
June

七月
chut yuet
July

八月
ba yuet
August

九月
gou yuet
September

十月
sup yuet
October

十一月
sup yut yuet
November

十二月
sup yi yuet
December

Seasons

季節

春季
chuun guai
Spring

夏季
ha guai
Summer

秋季
chou guai
Autumn/Fall

冬季
dung guai
Winter

季候風
guai hou fung
Monsoon

Days of the Week

星期天

星期一
xing kei yut
Monday

星期二
xing kei yi
Tuesday

星期三
xing kei saam
Wednesday

星期四
xing kei sei
Thursday

星期五
xing kei um
Friday

星期六
xing kei luk
Saturday

星期日
xing kei yaat
Sunday

Telling the Time

確認時間

時鐘
si zhung
clock

日間
yaat gaan
day

夜晚
ye maan
night

早上
jo sheung
morning

晚上
maan sheung
evening

手錶
sou biu
watch

十五分
sup um fun
quarter past

三十分
saan sup fun
half past

四十五分
sei sup um fun
quarter to

Colours

顔色

紅色
hung sek
red

橙色
chaang sek
orange

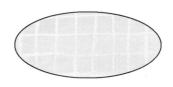

黃色
wong sek
yellow

綠色
luk sek
green

黑色
haak sek
black

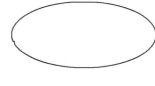

白色
baak sek
white

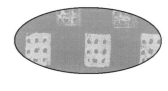

灰色
fui sek
grey

藍色
laam sek
blue

紫色
zhi sek
purple

粉紅色
fun hung sek
pink

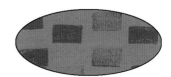

棕色
zhong sek
brown

Shapes

形狀

圓形
yuen ying
circle

星形
xing ying
star

三角形
saam gok ying
triangle

橢圓形
tor yuen ying
oval

圓錐形
yuen zui ying
cone

長方形
cheung fong ying
rectangle

四方形
sei fong ying
square

Numbers 1-20

1 　一
yut
one

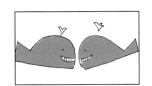
2 　二
yi
two

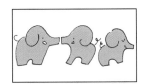
3 　三
saam
three

4 　四
sei
four

5 　五
um
five

6 　六
luk
six

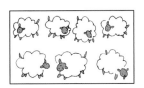
7 　七
chut
seven

8 　八
baat
eight

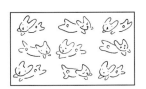
9 　九
gou
nine

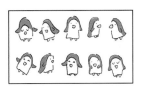
10 　十
sup
ten

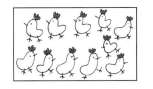
11 　十一
suo yut
eleven

12 　十二
sup yi
twelve

13 　十三
sup saam
thirteen

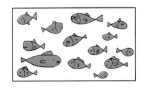
14 　十四
sup sei
fourteen

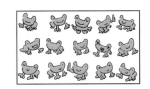
15 　十五
sup um
fifteen

16 　十六
sup luk
sixteen

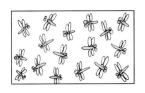
17 　十七
sup chut
seventeen

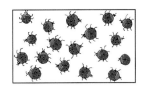
18 　十八
sup baat
eighteen

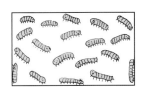
19 　十九
sup gou
nineteen

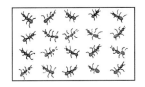
20 　二十
yi sup
twenty

Opposites

快
fai
fast

慢
maan
slow

開放
hoi fong
open

關閉
guaan bigh
closed

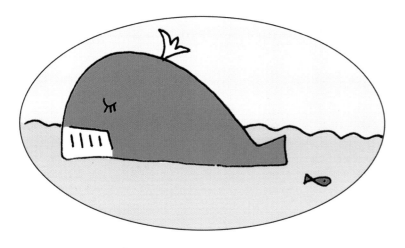

大
dai
large

小
siu
small

濕
sup
wet

乾
gone
dry

熱
yeet
hot

冷
leng
cold

甜
teem
sweet

酸
suen
sour

近
gun
near

遠
yuen
far

左
zhor
left

右
yao
right

前面
cheen meen
front

後面
hou meen
back

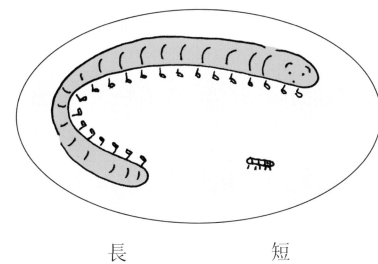

長
cheung
long

短
duen
short

重
chung
heavy

輕
hing
light

空
hung
empty

滿
moon
full

Index

Search for a word by picture or by the English word

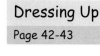

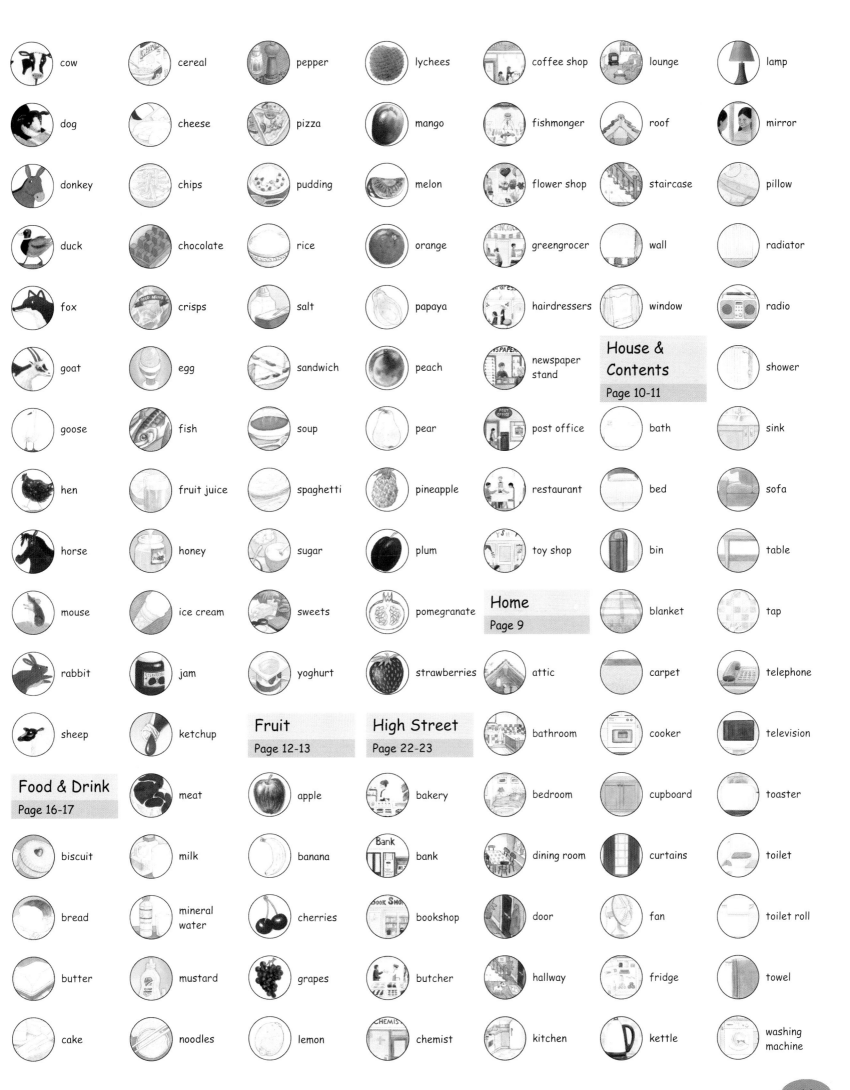

cow	cereal	pepper	lychees	coffee shop	lounge	lamp
dog	cheese	pizza	mango	fishmonger	roof	mirror
donkey	chips	pudding	melon	flower shop	staircase	pillow
duck	chocolate	rice	orange	greengrocer	wall	radiator
fox	crisps	salt	papaya	hairdressers	window	radio
goat	egg	sandwich	peach	newspaper stand	**House & Contents** Page 10-11	shower
goose	fish	soup	pear	post office	bath	sink
hen	fruit juice	spaghetti	pineapple	restaurant	bed	sofa
horse	honey	sugar	plum	toy shop	bin	table
mouse	ice cream	sweets	pomegranate	**Home** Page 9	blanket	tap
rabbit	jam	yoghurt	strawberries	attic	carpet	telephone
sheep	ketchup	**Fruit** Page 12-13	**High Street** Page 22-23	bathroom	cooker	television
Food & Drink Page 16-17	meat	apple	bakery	bedroom	cupboard	toaster
biscuit	milk	banana	bank	dining room	curtains	toilet
bread	mineral water	cherries	bookshop	door	fan	toilet roll
butter	mustard	grapes	butcher	hallway	fridge	towel
cake	noodles	lemon	chemist	kitchen	kettle	washing machine

61

Meal Time
Page 18-19

bowl
chopsticks
cup
flask
fork
frying pan
glass
knife
lunchbox
mug
plate
saucepan
spoon
wok

Months of the Year
Page 54

January
February
March
April
May
June
July
August
September
October
November
December

Music
Page 48-49

clarinet
drum
flute
gan gan
guitar
harp
keyboard
maracas
musical triangle
music stand
piano
recorder
tabla
trumpet
violin
xylophone

Myself
Page 4-5

angry
ankle
arm
back
ears
elbow
excited
eyes
face
feet
fingers
hair
hand
happy
head
hungry
jealous
knee
leg
mouth
neck
nose
sad
scared
shoulders
shy
sick
stomach
teeth
thumb
tired
toes
waist
wrist

Numbers 1-20
Page 57

one
two
three
four
five
six
seven
eight
nine
ten
eleven
twelve
thirteen
fourteen
fifteen
sixteen
seventeen
eighteen
nineteen
twenty

Opposites
Page 58-59

back
closed
cold
dry
empty
far
fast
front
full
heavy
hot
large
left
light
long
near

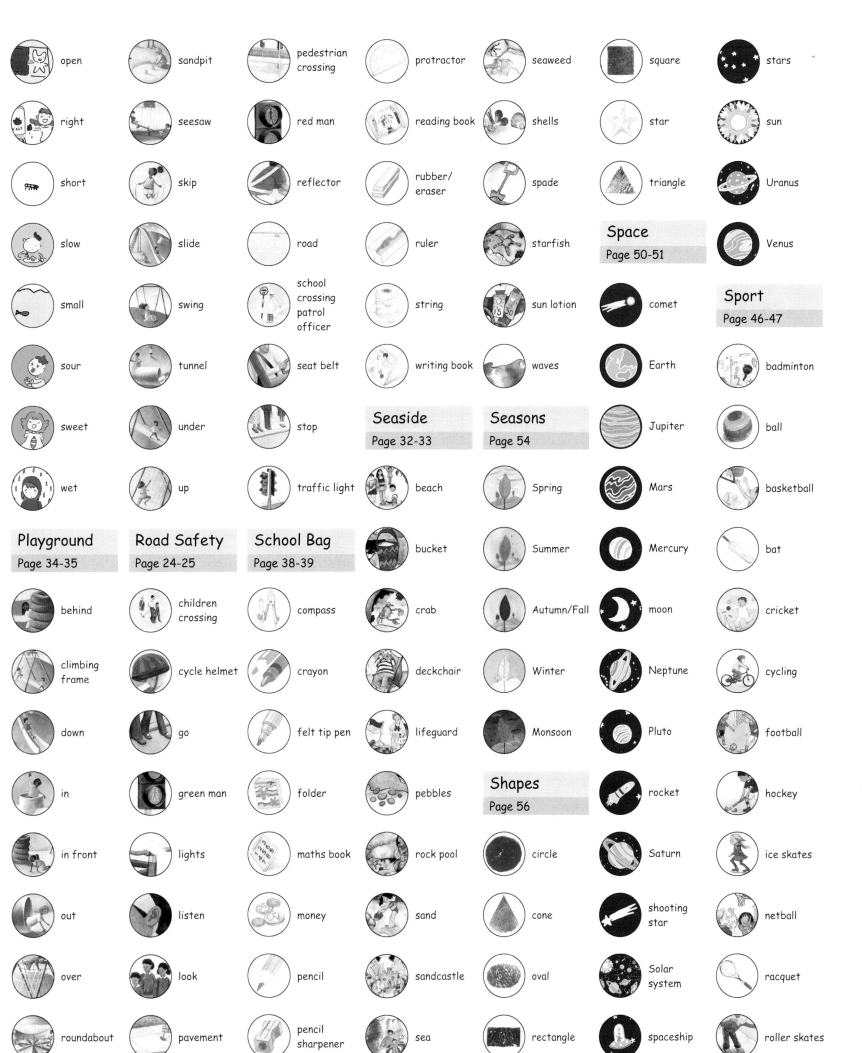

open

right

short

slow

small

sour

sweet

wet

Playground
Page 34-35

behind

climbing frame

down

in

in front

out

over

roundabout

sandpit

seesaw

skip

slide

swing

tunnel

under

up

Road Safety
Page 24-25

children crossing

cycle helmet

go

green man

lights

listen

look

pavement

pedestrian crossing

red man

reflector

road

school crossing patrol officer

seat belt

stop

traffic light

School Bag
Page 38-39

compass

crayon

felt tip pen

folder

maths book

money

pencil

pencil sharpener

protractor

reading book

rubber/ eraser

ruler

string

writing book

Seaside
Page 32-33

beach

bucket

crab

deckchair

lifeguard

pebbles

rock pool

sand

sandcastle

sea

seaweed

shells

spade

starfish

sun lotion

waves

Seasons
Page 54

Spring

Summer

Autumn/Fall

Winter

Monsoon

Shapes
Page 56

circle

cone

oval

rectangle

square

star

triangle

Space
Page 50-51

comet

Earth

Jupiter

Mars

Mercury

moon

Neptune

Pluto

rocket

Saturn

shooting star

Solar system

spaceship

stars

sun

Uranus

Venus

Sport
Page 46-47

badminton

ball

basketball

bat

cricket

cycling

football

hockey

ice skates

netball

racquet

roller skates

rugby
 cinema
 chess
 boat
 cucumber
 foggy
 crocodile

 skateboard
 fire station
 dice
 bus
 garlic
 hail
 dolphin

 swimming
 garage
 doll
 car
 lettuce
 icy
 elephant

 tennis
 hospital
 doll's house
 caravan
 mushroom
 lightning
 giraffe

Telling the Time
Page 55

 library
 kite
 coach
 onion
 rainbow
 hippopotamus

 clock
 park
 marbles
 helicopter
 peas
 rainy
 lion

 day
 police station
 playing cards
 lorry/truck
 pepper/capsicum
 snowy
 monkey

 evening
 school
 puppet
 motorbike
 potato
 stormy
 panda bear

 half past
 shops/stores
 puzzle
 rickshaw
 pumpkin/squash
 sunny
penguin

 morning
 sports centre
 skipping rope
 ship
 radish
 thunder
 shark

 night
 supermarket
 spinning top
 train
 sweetcorn
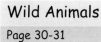 windy
 snake

 quarter past
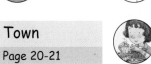 train station
 teddy bear
 tram
 tomato

Wild Animals
Page 30-31

 tiger

 quarter to

Toys and Games
Page 44-45

 train set

Vegetables
Page 14-15

Weather
Page 52-53

bear
 whale

 watch
 balloon
toy car
beans
cloudy
camel
 zebra

Town
Page 20-21

beads

Transport
Page 26-27

broccoli

bus station
board game
aeroplane
carrot

car park
building blocks
bicycle
cauliflower